Lisa Evans

STAMPING, SHOUTING AND SINGING HOME

For Dot, thank you

OBERON BOOKS
LONDON

WWW.OBERONBOOKS.COM

First published in 1988 by Methuen Drama
Published in 2006 by Oberon Books Ltd
521 Caledonian Road, London N7 9RH
Tel: +44 (0) 20 7607 3637 / Fax: +44 (0) 20 7607 3629
e-mail: info@oberonbooks.com
www.oberonbooks.com

A catalogue record for this book is available from the British
Library.

PB ISBN: 9781840027037
E ISBN: 9781786823250

Cover design by Corbis Images UK, Ltd

Visit www.oberonbooks.com to read more about all our books and to buy
them. You will also find features, author interviews and news of any author
events, and you can sign up for e-newsletters so that you're always first to
hear about our new releases.

Characters

PERFORMER 1
Lizzie

PERFORMER 2
Marguerite, Sojourner

PERFORMER 3
Mama, Louella

PERFORMER 4
Uncle Chrystal, Joanne, Teacher,
Preacher, Heckler, Cop

Setting:
On stage there are two trunks: one costume, one tin.

Stamping, Shouting and Singing Home was commissioned and first performed by Watford Palace Theatre-in-Education Company in 1986 with the following cast:

LIZZIE, Clare Perkins

MARGUERITE / SOJOURNER TRUTH, Vinny Dhillon

MAMA / LOUELLA, Janice McKenzie

UNCLE CHRYSTAL / JOANNE, Fiona Branson

Directed by Gwenda Hughes

Designed by Nettie Scriven

Musical Director Andrew Dodge

Stage Manager Gavin Stride

Administration Dot Butcher

ACT ONE

Scene 1

Song: 'Let My People Go.'

LIZZIE: The time, it is summer. The place, oh someplace in
the deep south. And the story? Been told before, be told
again. And I, knee high to a bug, walk, feet bare, step step
down the dusty track past the fields humming with Sunday
quiet. And the singing, so's their hearts would break,
coming from the black folks' church, as I slip away past the
hot sun and into the wood. And ain't I grown enough to
walk alone? Lord, you could be buried in the green in this
swampy place. Summer's been growing along a month or
so now. Out among the cotton it's as hot as Africa where
the stories come, so Mama tells it. The time, the beginning,
the place, my home, and me – Lizzie Walker – picking
flowers like there's no tomorrow. Look at the bunch I got
me already. Can't hear the singing no more, close in the
wood. Hum to myself instead, picking the silver ferns and
flowers blue as white folks' eyes. Hear my mama saying…

MAMA: You watch out for snakes now, you hear?

LIZZIE: Stop by this big ole tree, bark all mossy green and
damp. Been here since before the Indians even, I reckon.
If there was such a time. Looking up I sees the patchwork
pieces of sky. Seems God left a thread dangling. Hanging
frayed from a branch. It was then his foot touched my
cheek. Except it wasn't like no foot I ever seen – just bones
charred black. The bones of what was once his hands
outstretched like he's still begging for life. Big hands. A
working man. Could have been a brother. Necklace of
barbed wire still clinging round his jaw as he swings gentle,
what was once a man, over what was once a fire. He
should be buried proper. Seem like his story over and done
with sure enough. Sure enough summer over too.

Song: 'Let My People Go.'

7

Scene 2

*As LIZZIE speaks she unpacks key props/items of clothing from the trunk
and hands them to the other performers.*

LIZZIE: And here I am now, unpacking the past. Trunk full
of history, old clothes my family wore I can't bear to
throw away. The attic's full of them. And a feather duster
my Great Uncle Chrystal used for the training of cats.
Marguerite's scarf, Mama's pinafore and this jacket. Well, it
belonged to my big brother Charles. Only he's dead now.
He was killed fighting across the world. But you'll get to
hear about him all the same. In my family there's dead folk
hopping in and outa the conversation all the time. Mama
would sit in her rocker, wrapped in her shawl, sewing the
quilt and telling tales of my great-granma and her mama,
Sojourner Truth, and sisters stretching back in time, way
back, across the seas to Africa where we began. So many
sisters, so many stories. And my sister, whose middle name
was Trouble. But we generally called her Marguerite. She
was bigger than me and badder than me and she answered
back all the time and got away with it. Mama'd say.

MAMA: You just like your great-great-granma, Sojourner Truth.

LIZZIE: Wasn't nobody got the better of Sojourner, spite the
fact she born a slave who never learned to read nor write.
And then there was me, Lizzie Walker, just trying to reach
a mark a bit higher up the barn door each summer. Just
trying to get along on my own story without any trouble.
Let me tell you one thing, sure enough, that ain't easy
coming youngest in a long line of wilful women. Seems
once folk gotten into the way of being active, it's awful
hard keeping them down.

Scene 3

MAMA: Lizzie, Marguerite, you ready for school?

LIZZIE/MARGUERITE: Yes Mama.

MAMA: School teaches you how to think. You lucky we allowed a school for coloured folk. Off you go now.

Song: 'Battle Hymn of the Republic' as first MARGUERITE and then LIZZIE move to school.

TEACHER: You all pay attention now. Lizzie Walker, you're late again. Dreaming I suppose.

LIZZIE: No Ma'am.

TEACHER: Today is history. H-I-S-T-O-R-Y.

MARGUERITE: Lizzie.

TEACHER: John Brown. B-R-O-W-N.

LIZZIE: What?

MARGUERITE: There's a cockroach heading up your skirt.

LIZZIE: Where!

TEACHER: Lizzie Walker, what are you doing?

LIZZIE: Just looking, Ma'am.

TEACHER: Well don't. What do you know about John Brown?

MARGUERITE: (*Singing.*) His body lies a mouldering in the grave but his soul goes marching on. Ma'am.

TEACHER: I won't have no singing of that kind here. John Brown was a fanatic. A traitor. Who knows what that means?

MARGUERITE: He's bad, Ma'am?

TEACHER: Yes Marguerite. He was a crazy man. He talked poor coloured men who didn't know no better, into a riot. They were shot by the forces of law and order.

LIZZIE: I don't see no roach.

TEACHER: Lizzie Walker!

LIZZIE: Yes Ma'am.

TEACHER: What is law and order?

LIZZIE: Doing as you're told, Ma'am?

TEACHER: Mm. By who?

LIZZIE: White folks?

TEACHER: By the sheriff, the state police and the government.

MARGUERITE: (*To LIZZIE.*) That's white folks.

LIZZIE: Oh.

MARGUERITE: Your roach gone marching up your back, Lizzie.

LIZZIE: Where?

MARGUERITE: I see his whiskers waving.

LIZZIE: Marguerite, if you telling me stories, you going to go to hell.

MARGUERITE: It's the truth.

TEACHER: He was hanged on December the Second, 1859 by the neck until he was dead.

LIZZIE: I can't see it.

MARGUERITE: Waving his legs now. About to bite your ear, poison your blood.

LIZZIE leaps up screeching and flapping.

TEACHER: Lizzie Walker, you come here to learn, not to fool around!

LIZZIE: She said I had a cockroach up my back, Ma'am. I couldn't sit still knowing he marching up and down my spine.

TEACHER: I'll give you marching, right out of this class! Let me see.

MARGUERITE: It was a roach.

TEACHER: Marguerite, you telling lies?

MARGUERITE: No Ma'am, there was a roach, swear to God.

TEACHER: Sit down, Lizzie and you pay attention, Marguerite. I am attempting to teach you history. That's spelled H-I-S – Marguerite?

MARGUERITE: His.

TEACHER: Then story. His story. What's that?

MARGUERITE: It's the truth Ma'am. Written in books, like the Bible and all.

TEACHER: And the people who wrote these books were people who knew. Clever people. People in command of the facts. Class dismissed.

LIZZIE/MARGUERITE: Thank you Miss Wescott.

LIZZIE: Please Ma'am?

TEACHER: What is it?

LIZZIE: Did black folks ever write these books, history?

TEACHER: How could they, most of them couldn't read nor write?

LIZZIE: Oh.

MARGUERITE: Come on.

MARGUERITE and LIZZIE move away.

TEACHER leaves.

LIZZIE: Was there really a roach?

MARGUERITE: Yes.

LIZZIE: You be going to get struck by a thunderbolt if you lie.

MARGUERITE: I seen him, scuttling across the floor.

LIZZIE: And?

MARGUERITE: I didn't tell her no lie. I just said there was a
roach. That's the truth.

LIZZIE: What about when it done run up my back?

MARGUERITE: I didn't tell the teacher that.

LIZZIE: You told me!

MARGUERITE: I sort of imagined what the roach might do if it
had a mind.

LIZZIE: It's just as well you can't write good yet, Marguerite.
Cos you put that down in letters and sure as hell you going
to get hit by that thunderbolt. Blow you further up the road
than a cottonball in the wind.

Song: 'John Brown's Body'.

*In between the verses as the tin bath is brought out, LIZZIE
speaks.*

In the next part of my story I ain't got no clothes and this is
full of water.

LIZZIE climbs fully dressed into the empty bath.

Scene 4

MARGUERITE is drying her hair. MAMA is washing a reluctant LIZZIE in the tin tub.

MAMA: And like Sojourner's Mama say to her, I say to you, see the stars, those are the same stars and that is the same moon that look down upon your brothers and sisters, and which they see as they look up at them though they ever so far away from us and each other. For her brothers and sisters were sold away from home to other slave owners before they even as big as you. And when she nine years old Sojourner she sold away from home too, to a man who bought her along with a flock of sheep. A man who gave her no shoes so her feet froze like the river in winter. While Sojourner sleeping on straw and crying for cold, her Mama done die and, big deal, Sojourner allowed to go visit her Pa for the funeral. Just one day though and back to work and being beaten day and night with rods tied together. One day she gets sold, for seventy dollars cos she a good worker, better than a man, her master say. She washing all the white family's clothes in the night time and hoeing and raking in the fields all day. This new master look at Sojourner, big and strong, and he thinks 'this slave be right for breeding'. So he picks one of his men slaves and he says, 'I decided, you two married now.' And in time Sojourner, she have five children, five new brown workers. But things is changing. The law says on July the Fourth Sojourner going to be free. She wait so eager for this day but when it come, the Master say, 'You was sick a while back. You gotta make up that time afore I set you free.' Suddenly, been told before, be told again, Sojourner see the light. He ain't never going to free her. So she pick up the smallest baby with one arm and a bundle of belongings with the other and she run away. Sojourner learned, ain't no good sitting and waiting on some master to give you freedom. You got to take it.

And then, like Harriet, you got to give it away to other brothers and sisters, time and time again.

LIZZIE is now out of the bath and being dried.

LIZZIE: Who were Harriet and Sojourner, Mama, are they history?

MAMA: Yes.

LIZZIE: Then why ain't they in the books?

MAMA: Lots of ordinary folks got left out, honey. They still there – like Sojourner speaking her truth and Harriet Tubman setting folks free.

LIZZIE: And I looked at the history books and found she was right. Nobody wrote nothing about me and my kind. Seemed like someone decided we didn't exist. Goes to show how wrong some people can be.

Scene 5

On the veranda. TWO WHITE WOMEN sip cold drinks served to them by MARGUERITE.

LOUELLA: I don't know what's the matter in this town today, really I don't.

JOANNE: Mary, don't forget the shirts must be starched again. My husband is very particular.

MARGUERITE: Yes Ma'am.

MARGUERITE exits.

LOUELLA: They're getting so uppity. Grinning from ear to ear. Our menfolks won't stand for it. There'll be trouble tonight, mark my words, Joanne. Mark my words.

JOANNE: It's all on account of that fight I daresay. Like children.

LOUELLA: My, this heat's enough to tire a body out.

They sip their drinks.

JOANNE: Mary! There's not enough sugar in this. Mary!

MARGUERITE enters wiping her hands.

MARGUERITE: Yes Ma'am?

JOANNE: Don't come to the table wiping your hands, Mary. Sugar.

MARGUERITE: You said you wanted less, for the weight Ma'am.

JOANNE: Don't cheek me, girl.

MARGUERITE: No Ma'am.

MARGUERITE exits.

JOANNE: Mary! Cussedness! Mary! When I took her on, out of the goodness of my heart, she tells me her name's Marguerite, or some such foolishness.

LOUELLA: Marguerite! My they do have such fancy names.

JOANNE: Too fancy. And too long. I can't be shouting Marguerite all day long. So I call her Mary. It's simpler.

LOUELLA: What fight were you talking about, Joanne dear? In the street here in town? I didn't hear nothing.

MARGUERITE enters.

JOANNE: Some boy won some boxing fight, that's all. Everyone reckoned the title holder would win, then back comes this Louis, hits him for the count.

LOUELLA: Was he a black?

JOANNE: Yes. Mary, why didn't you answer me?

MARGUERITE: Ma'am?

JOANNE: I have better ways to spend my time than call after you.

LOUELLA: What was that black boy's name?

MARGUERITE: Joe Louis, Ma'am! The sugar.

MARGUERITE puts down the sugar bowl and sweeps the yard.

JOANNE: If she wasn't such a hard worker I'd have fired her weeks ago.

JOANNE ladles sugar into her drink.

MARGUERITE: Into the ring. Round one.

JOANNE: Sugar, Louella?

LOUELLA: No thank you dear. I can't abide fighting.

JOANNE takes a mouthful of the drink and chokes.

There there dear.

JOANNE: (*Gasping.*) Salt. She brought salt!

LOUELLA: Oh dear. Mary! Mary, bring some water for your mistress, you wicked girl!

MARGUERITE: Round two! He's off the ropes, ladies and gentlemen. He's moving up towards the centre of the ring.

LOUELLA: Fetch water, girl!

MARGUERITE: And now it looks like Louis getting mad. There's a left cross and a right to the head.

LOUELLA: She's gone stone crazy, Joanne.

MARGUERITE: Eight, nine, ten – and it's Joe Louis the winner and Heavyweight Champion of the World!

JOANNE: Stop it at once, Mary!

MARGUERITE: Ma'am.

JOANNE: You are going to get such a whipping for this Mary.

LOUELLA: A whipping, do you hear?

JOANNE: Fetch the switch, Mary. And one word from you and you'll be leaving, not just here but town. Isn't nobody going to give you work if I say not.

MARGUERITE: Yes Ma'am.

LOUELLA: It shouldn't be allowed. It gives them ideas. Champion of the World indeed.

JOANNE: I'm going to tame you good and proper.

MARGUERITE: No Ma'am. You going to tame Mary. My name's Marguerite.

Song: 'No More Moaning'.

Scene 6

At home. MARGUERITE enters. LIZZIE watches the following scene, bringing MAMA the bowl and cloth to bathe MARGUERITE's back.

MAMA: You gave her salt instead of sugar?

MARGUERITE: Yes.

MAMA: A mistake?

MARGUERITE: Mn hm.

MAMA: C'mon over here, Trouble.

Matter of factly MAMA bathes MARGUERITE's back, her anger and what-to-do-about-it-all coming out in her positive story about HARRIET.

MARGUERITE: Ow.

MAMA: Hold still. Now the way the story goes, the overseer calls to Harriet, 'Stop that man! Runaway slave! I'm going to whip him till he know his place!' And Harriet see this

17

slave, head down and running. He goes past her and
through the door. A brother breaking free. Now Harriet,
she don't think, she just act. And she move in front of that
door, blocking the overseer's path. Stands like a rock. Mad
as hell, the overseer picks up a two pound weight and hurls
it. It catch Harriet square on her forehead knocking her
unconscious near to death. From harvest past Christmas
she lay in the slave cabin, not moving, like a stone. And
come spring she wake up and there begins the story
of another sister – Harriet Tubman – who ran away to
Canada and then came back, again and again. Dressed
as a man for a price higher than gold was on her head,
and lead her people along the riverbanks, cross miles of
slave-owning land, with dogs baying after them, in danger
and darkness. And all the while keeping their spirits going
with songs of freedom. And each time she come back she'd
whistle outside the cabins, low and quiet –

MAMA whistles two lines of 'Go Down Moses'.

– as a sign she'd come to lead more brothers and sisters
north out of slavery. And for this they called her Moses.
A small black woman with no learning and a deep hole in
her forehead marking the price she pay to say no for the
first time.

MARGUERITE: It don't hurt so much now, Mama.

MAMA: Salt instead of sugar huh?

Song: 'Oh Freedom'.

Scene 7

*MAMA is cutting up old pieces of material for her quilt. LIZZIE is reading
the Bible.*

LIZZIE: 'And the Lord said unto the woman, what is this that
thou hast done? I will greatly multiply thy sorrow.' What's
that one, Mama?

MAMA: That? I think it's your granma's wedding dress.

LIZZIE: But it's all patterns.

MAMA: She love your granpa just the same. Get along with your reading, Lizzie.

LIZZIE: 'Thy conception, in sorrow thou shalt bring forth children; and thy desire shall be to thy husband and he shall rule over thee.' What's rule, Mama?

MAMA: It's when one set of folks tells another set of folks what to do.

LIZZIE: Was Adam white?

MAMA: No child, he was just a man.

LIZZIE: Oh. Mama, why didn't God like Eve?

MAMA: She eaten of the Tree of Knowledge, she know too much. Go find your sister now.

LIZZIE: I been running around all day.

MAMA: Then walk. You got the name for it. Walker.

LIZZIE: I'm tired.

MAMA: And you ain't even started yet. Sojourner walked everywhere.

LIZZIE: Well I bet she got tired too sometimes.

MAMA: I reckon she did. Tired of hearing the same old excuses, same as I do!

LIZZIE: Tell me a story Mama. About Sojourner.

MAMA: Well…oh, you are one daughter of Eve and no mistake – real clever. But so am I. So go get Marguerite and then I'll tell you about how Sojourner stood up for old Eve. Now get along!

MAMA leaves.

Scene 8

LIZZIE: Marguerite! Marguerite!

Getting no response, LIZZIE starts to play hopscotch with an imaginary person. She goes first.

Your turn. And no cheating. Ah ah. My turn now, and I'm going to win.

MARGUERITE enters engrossed in a newspaper.

Mama wants you. She sent me out to get you.

MARGUERITE: I can see you been looking real hard.

LIZZIE: I'm winning.

She continues her game.

MARGUERITE: Who you playing with?

LIZZIE: Never you mind.

MARGUERITE: There's nobody there.

LIZZIE: Yes there is.

MARGUERITE: Who then?

LIZZIE: God.

MARGUERITE: You playing hopscotch against God!

LIZZIE: Yes. And I'm winning. Where you been?

MARGUERITE: Reading.

LIZZIE: Me too. All about how God give Eve a real hard time cos she went talking to a snake.

MARGUERITE goes back to reading her paper.

MARGUERITE: Uh huh.

LIZZIE: I wouldn't talk to no snake. Eve must have been real lonely talking to a dumb creature. I reckon Adam wasn't much good at passing the time of day. Probably too busy combing his hair like Charles.

MARGUERITE: What?

LIZZIE: Well, like Charles used to, fore he went to the war. Can't you just picture it? (*As Eve.*) Hi Adam, nice day. Looks like it might rain. Big storm clouds approaching over Eden. (*As Adam, combing his hair.*) Uh huh. (*As Eve.*) Yeah, I reckon that cloud going to break soon. Going to be one wet weekend in Eden all right. What d'ya say we go someplace else for the day? (*As Adam.*) Uh huh. (*As Eve.*) Course if you don't reckon much to that, we could just lie around here watching the apples fall off the tree. (*As Adam.*) Uh huh. (*As Eve.*) Or I guess I could just go talk to a snake. (*As Adam.*) OK. You do that. You listening, Marguerite?

MARGUERITE: Uh huh.

LIZZIE: So anyways, Eve has this real good conversation with this snake about how apples is good for your teeth and all. I spect she moans on a bit about how Adam spend all his time combing his hair and not paying her no attention…

MARGUERITE: There's going to be a march here in town.

LIZZIE: That right? Well, it's just coming on to evening and Eve sees she was right about the weather, sure enough. So she calls out to Adam, 'Hey Adam, it's going to rain like hell and you going to catch your death out there with no clothes on, you hear!' And WHAM! Down come God on a thunderbolt and kicks them out of their house in Eden and all cos Adam wasn't no good at making conversation. Whatcha think?

MARGUERITE: I think I ought to go.

LIZZIE: Go where?

MARGUERITE: On the march.

LIZZIE: You kidding? Folks gets in trouble for that. We got to get home.

MARGUERITE: No news about his regiment in the paper.

LIZZIE: (*Going back to playing hopscotch.*) Who?

MARGUERITE: Charles of course. Your brother, remember?

LIZZIE: Oh yeah, that Charles. I spect he going to come home a hero anyways.

MARGUERITE: Just so long as he come home.

LIZZIE: What for? So's he can pull your hair again and twist your arm fit to break? I don't care if he never come back.

MARGUERITE shakes LIZZIE.

MARGUERITE: Don't you ever dare say that again, Lizzie Walker, you hear me?!

LIZZIE: Let me go!

MARGUERITE: He's your brother.

LIZZIE: So? You my sister and you shaking me to bits. What's so fine about brothers and sisters?

MARGUERITE: Ask Mama.

LIZZIE: I shall so too.

MARGUERITE leaves.

Like I said, just being dead don't keep you out of family conversation. Fact is, you probably gets more air time that way. Like Sojourner and her chosen name of Truth.

LIZZIE gets the patchwork quilt and helps MAMA unfold it.

Scene 9

LIZZIE listens as MAMA tells the story.

MAMA: And when Sojourner enter the meeting hall they all turns and looks. Six feet tall of woman and black woman at that, in her Quaker bonnet and long skirts.

SOJOURNER enters.

She look at the speakers sitting up on the platform and at the crowd assembled and something ain't right. They supposed to be talking about women's rights and all the folks who are talking and hollering is men, and church men at that. And they say…

WHITE HECKLER: If God wanted the equality of women he'd have made them strong as men! Jesus was a man! It was Eve caused Adam to be thrown out of Eden!

MAMA: Now Sojourner, she keep quiet for one whole day of this nonsense. Come day two, she rise slowly to her feet and move to the centre of the platform. They try to stop her with their shouting. But Sojourner got something to say. She silence them with one long look.

SOJOURNER: Well children, where there is so much racket there must be something out of kilter. Between the negroes in the South and the white women in the North all talking about rights, you white men will be in a fix pretty soon. But what's all this talking about?

MAMA: At which they starts shouting again.

WHITE HECKLER: If women need seats in carriages and strong arms to help them they don't need rights!

MAMA: Sojourner's eyes flash like thunderbolts.

SOJOURNER: That man over there says that women need to be helped into carriages and lifted over ditches, and to have the best place everywhere. Nobody ever helps me into carriages, or over mud puddles, or gives me any best place, and ain't I a woman? Look at me! Look at my arm! I have ploughed and planted and gathered into barns, and no man could head me – and ain't I a woman? I could work as much and eat as much as a man (when I could get it) and bear the lash as well – and ain't I a woman? I have borne five children and seen them most all sold off into slavery, and when I cried out with a mother's grief, none but Jesus heard – and ain't I a woman?

MAMA: And ain't I a woman?

WHITE HECKLER: Jesus was a man!

SOJOURNER: Jesus was born from God and a woman. Man had nothing to do with it.

MAMA: She got him there.

WHITE HECKLER: What about Eve and the serpent. Women is trouble!

MAMA: You bet she got an answer for that too.

SOJOURNER: If the first woman God ever made was strong enough to turn the world upside down, all alone, all these women here together ought to be able to turn it back and get it right side up again, and now they're asking to do it…

MAMA: The men better let them!

LIZZIE: Well, if Mama and Sojourner thought old Eve was one fine woman, far as I concerned, she was. You know, seems to me Joe Louis, Champion Fighter and Sojourner Truth got a lot in common. And on account of the stories, which kept on coming, the fighting didn't stop there. Like the evening sister Marguerite didn't come home. It was a Saturday, always a bad night as Mama did the accounts.

Scene 10

MAMA is doing the accounts. LIZZIE has a bag of sweets and is reading the Bible.

MAMA: Milk, meal, cornstarch makes three dollars twenty. We going to have to cut down.

LIZZIE: I knew where Marguerite been going, but I wasn't telling. Not me.

MAMA: Where is that girl, it's past nightfall?

LIZZIE: Who Mama?

MAMA: Don't you act womanish with me Lizzie Walker.

LIZZIE: Me, Mama? I was really living dangerous. I pretended to be reading but I could feel Mama's eyes boring holes in the top of my head. It gone real quiet.

MAMA: Lizzie.

LIZZIE: Yes Mama?

MAMA: Tell me the part of the Bible you learned yesterday.

LIZZIE: Her voice like oil. Better watch out. Which part Mama?

MAMA: About how the first wrote.

LIZZIE: 'The first wrote, wine is the strongest
The second wrote, the King is strongest
The third wrote, women are strongest'
I liked that. I was strong. I wasn't telling no tales.

MAMA: Wasn't there another line?

LIZZIE: Was there?

MAMA. I think so, don't you?

LIZZIE: She got me.
'But above all things Truth beareth away the victory'

MAMA: So where is Marguerite?

LIZZIE: Now there's times when you just got to stand your ground.

MAMA: Lizzie.

LIZZIE: I don't know.

MAMA: Elizabeth.

LIZZIE: And times you just got to admit defeat. Down the white folks' end of town.

MAMA: And you sat here all evening knowing this and never saying a word?

LIZZIE: I promised.

MAMA: Hold your tongue! Doesn't she know how dangerous that is? She been sleepwalking all her life? Saturday night and the white men out in their cars drinking and looking for trouble. Well, doesn't she know?

LIZZIE: Marguerite said…

MAMA: Don't answer me back!

LIZZIE: (*To audience.*) How come it's Marguerite's done wrong and I'm the one getting hollered at?

MAMA: Don't she know she crying out for trouble? That girl got less sense than a nodding dog. And as for you!

LIZZIE: It was about this time I got real interested in my reading.

Her head is virtually inside her Bible.

MAMA: And she went out wearing nothing but a thin dress. If she come home, please Lord, soaked through with pneumonia, she needn't think I'm going to sit up day and night nursing her. Oh no.

LIZZIE: I could tell we in for a bumpy night. Mama putting on her going-into-battle-hat.

MAMA: I prayed to the Lord to send me children and what do I get? Chicken brains, that's what! Charles playing soldiers and shooting at yellow people halfway cross the world, Marguerite gallivanting around all night where she didn't ought to be, getting herself beat up and run over, taking to drink and being abused...

LIZZIE: Mama, you don't know that for sure.

MAMA: Don't you tell me what I know! She lying murdered in some ditch this very minute for certain. And then she going to walk home alone on that road in the pitch dark. When she come in, please Lord, I'm going to give her such a hiding she won't know Thursday from Christmas.

LIZZIE: Shall I read to you Mama?

MAMA: Yes.

MAMA doesn't listen.

LIZZIE: 'And in the time of their visitation they shall shine, and run to and fro like sparks among the stubble. And so...'

MARGUERITE enters.

Marguerite!

MAMA: Baby, where have you been?

LIZZIE: And Marguerite she just stands there in the doorway, rain or something running down her cheeks, clothes clinging to her bones like a cat someone tried to drown. And she don't say nothing.

MAMA puts the quilt around MARGUERITE.

MAMA. Are you hurt?

MARGUERITE shakes her head.

Did anyone abuse you, child?

MARGUERITE shakes her head.

Well where in the name of heaven you been?!

LIZZIE: Mama about to start blowing like the wind whistling
outside when something in Marguerite's look stops her.
Seems like it's my sister's turn to tell her story.

MARGUERITE: I went to the coffee shop.

MAMA: But that's a white folks' place.

MARGUERITE: Law says it isn't.

MAMA: Law! Why, honey?

MARGUERITE: I wanted to drink coffee.

LIZZIE: What happened?

MAMA: Ssh. Let her tell it like it was.

MARGUERITE: I didn't plan on staying out late Mama. It
was light when I went in. It was real crowded but only
a few folks sitting outside at them pretty tables on the
sidewalk. So I went and sat there too. Folks were staring
like I come from Mars or someplace. You think my skin
green not brown. But I didn't take notice. I sat at the table
and waited for the waitress. Pretty soon she come out and
took an order from the table next to mine. Then she goes
back inside. Through the glass I could see white folks
nudging and laughing at me, and the waitress talking to the
manager. She come out with the order for the next table.
This time I say, 'Excuse me Miss.' But she act like I wasn't
there. No voice. No sound. But I heard my voice. And I
heard it again when next she pass and I say, very polite,
'I'd like a cup of coffee, please.' I ask three more times but
she carries on acting like I'm invisible. Then it come on to
rain. But I sat on. I sat on while it got dark and they turned
up the lights inside. And folks came and went and had
coffee and cake and talked and laughed together. And I sat

on. Pretending I didn't care. They weren't going to drive me away. Flood could have come and I'd have stayed, sitting in the dark, rain on the window panes, running down my back till I didn't rightly know if I was turned to stone. Some cars hooted as they drove off, laughing and yelling foul words. But I sat on. I had a right to be sitting there. I had a right to be served coffee just like they did. So I sat on. Then they closed up, put out the lights. I got up and come home.

LIZZIE looks in her bag of sweets. There is one left. She gives it to MARGUERITE.

Song: 'Hush You Bye'.

End of Act One.

ACT TWO

Scene 1

Song: 'Take This Hammer'.

LIZZIE: My great-great-granma was a slave and all her family
too and the way they taught me in school they all had a
pretty good time of it. A place to live, all their food and
plenty of smiling black folks picking cotton and singing
along under the Southern sun.

Song: first verse of 'She Know Moon-rise', sung by all.

SONG: Our Rit'll walk in the starlight
She'll walk in the starlight
To lay her body down.

LIZZIE: And so the season's went past with no worries and no
responsibilities. Seedtime, Cotton Blossom Time, Harvest
and Christmas. All in the service of King Cotton.

SONG: Our Rit'll walk in the graveyard
She'll walk through the graveyard
To lay her body down.

LIZZIE: And yet and still they taught me the slaves kept on
smiling, praising the Lord, picking the fleecy white cotton
and keeping the big houses with their wide verandas so
clean they ready for white-glove inspection.

SONG: Our Rit'll lie in the graveyard
Stretch out her arms in the graveyard
To lay her body down.

LIZZIE: Truth beareth away the victory. If you can't dance it
and you can't sing it, leastways it ought to be told right.
When my granma got active those white men come and
dug up her ma's grave. Dumped her dust in the front yard.
Found a splinter of finger bone among the marigolds.

I'll tell it and tell it right. You see, I owe it, to those who walked before and those on the road to come.

SONG: She know moon-rise
She know star-rise
But she done lay her body down.

LIZZIE: Truth was, things beginning to hot up. Marguerite's getting active, causing trouble. Mind, she'd been that way since I could remember. Since she started telling me I had cockroaches crawling down my back. Now though it was other folks she got scratching. Like the day Miz Joanne come home from the hospital and got bit by the snake.

Scene 2

LOUELLA and JOANNE are lolling on the veranda fanning themselves.

LOUELLA: How many pints you say you lost Joanne?

JOANNE: Altogether I had to be given thirteen pints of blood.

LOUELLA: All at the same time?

JOANNE: Don't be foolish, Louella. Thirteen wouldn't fit all at once.

LOUELLA: I was wondering. You'd have looked like a bullfrog.

JOANNE: I have been a very sick woman Louella, kindly don't upset me with your jokes.

MARGUERITE enters carrying a bunch of herbs and speaks to LOUELLA.

MARGUERITE: Morning Ma'am.

JOANNE: Where have you been Mary? I've been calling and calling.

MARGUERITE: How you doing Ma'am?

LOUELLA: Thank you, just fine.

JOANNE: Mary, I asked you a question!

MARGUERITE: I'll just take these herbs on down to the kitchen.

JOANNE: Mary!

MARGUERITE exits.

LOUELLA: Don't you go upsetting yourself now, Joanne. You're a sick woman. Eleven pints remember.

JOANNE: Thirteen. I had thirteen. And all of it white.

LOUELLA: No Joanne dear. Blood's red.

JOANNE: I said to them as they were putting the needle in my arm. No black blood. I die first. Then I saw the needle and fainted clean away. I've always been of a delicate nature you know. MARY!

LOUELLA: I'm wondering if perhaps the sun's too strong out on the porch Joanne dear.

JOANNE: I need a drop of Southern Comfort for my strength. MARY!

LOUELLA: Now quieten down dear. I'll fetch her. You rest up.

JOANNE: Oh very well.

LOUELLA: (*Quietly.*) Marguerite?

MARGUERITE appears instantly with a drink.

MARGUERITE: Yes Ma'am?

LOUELLA: Miss Joanne would like a glass of spirits.

MARGUERITE: She ain't allowed no strong liquor, doctor said.

MARGUERITE gives JOANNE the drink.

You have a sip of that Ma'am. Do you a power of good.

JOANNE: What is it?

MARGUERITE: To keep your spirits up.

JOANNE: (*Brightening.*) Spirit?

LOUELLA: (*Fanning herself.*) We all need our spirits up in these hard times. I declare we do.

JOANNE takes a mouthful and spits it out.

JOANNE: Take it away!

MARGUERITE: I know it tastes a little bitter, but it's real good for you Ma'am.

JOANNE: She's trying to poison me!

LOUELLA: Oh I shouldn't think so Joanne, she'd be out of a job if she did.

JOANNE: Take that away. I ain't drinking no poisonous witch's brew.

MARGUERITE: It's just herbs and roots to strengthen the blood Miz Joanne.

JOANNE: Don't talk to me about blood. I know. Thirteen pints and all of it white.

LOUELLA: Red dear.

JOANNE: Oh shut up!

LIZZIE: Well, what with all this talk about black blood, white blood and hospitals, no-one notices the moccasin snake sliding round the porch steps looking for a shady place in the cool.

JOANNE: Oh my God I've been bitten!

LOUELLA: A snake! It's there! A snake!

LIZZIE: Quick as a flash of sunlight, Marguerite picks up the broom and shoosh sends the moccasin snake flying off the porch and into the bushes.

JOANNE: I'm going to die!

LOUELLA: Oh lord. Oh lord.

MARGUERITE: Stop waving your arms around. You make the poison travel.

LIZZIE: And Marguerite puts the cut to her mouth and sucks hard. And spits out the poison, blood and all.

JOANNE: Savage!

LIZZIE: Marguerite rips a piece off of Miz Joanne's skirt.

JOANNE: My dress!

LIZZIE: And ties it onto her arm.

JOANNE: Ouch, you're hurting! It's too tight.

MARGUERITE: Miz Louella Ma'am, get down off of that chair and hold her arm real tight. Just here. Don't loosen up.

JOANNE: She drank my blood.

MARGUERITE: Just as likely to be mine Miz Joanne Ma'am. I been giving blood down that hospital since I been grown. And only label on the bottles is the blood group.

JOANNE: Oh my God, black blood!

LIZZIE: Marguerite got one more thing to say before she leave and don't come back.

MARGUERITE: You lie still while I wash my mouth. I sucked most of the snake poison out I think, but seems like you making your own poison right inside your head. Next time you get bitten, I reckon it's the snake going to need treatment. Goodbye.

Song: 'Little David Play On Your Harp'.

Scene 3

MAMA and MARGUERITE are doing the washing in the same tub LIZZIE was bathed in. LIZZIE runs on waving an airmail letter.

LIZZIE: Mama! It's a letter! From Charles!

MAMA: Is that so?

MARGUERITE: Aren't you going to open it?

MAMA wipes her hands carefully.

MAMA: In my own good time.

LIZZIE: You going to read it to us too?

MAMA: You carry on with that washing.

LIZZIE hangs out the washing.

(*Reading.*) 'Dear Mama, how are you? I am okay I guess. Remember Joshua Regan, enlisted same time as me? He went kinda crazy a while back and they're shipping him home today. Hope this reaches you. It seems a real long way away. The officers tell us we're winning, so I guess we are. Yesterday we entered the city, I'm not allowed to say which one. We followed the bombing our boys done from the air. They done a good job it's said, near flattened it. As we went in I saw a girl, bout Lizzie's age I guess, trapped in the rubble from the waist down. I stayed there. They told me she said she could feel with her feet the corpses of her parents. And still she kept on singing. She had short black hair and skinny yellow brown arms. She died this morning. I don't know which side she was on. It's very hot. They don't have Thanksgiving here, so no turkey. Your loving son, Charles. P.S. Her name was Miko.' Go fill up the can Marguerite. Time to water the garden.

MARGUERITE exits whistling 'John Brown's Body' softly.

LIZZIE: Whenever Mama felt real bad we'd go to church. Like our people done since time began we'd sing our tears and our hopes.

Scene 4

Church. MAMA, LIZZIE and MARGUERITE are there. PREACHER enters.

PREACHER: I will now call upon Lizzie Walker to lead the sisters and brothers in the singing of Swing Low Sweet Chariot.

LIZZIE: During slavery all that Swing Low Sweet Chariot coming for to carry me home wasn't about dying like the white folks thought. It meant, tonight we makes a break for it. Kinda code, Mama says.

LIZZIE sings 'Swing Low' alone.

PREACHER: Thank you Lizzie. And the Lord said, 'Let my people go. And if you refuse to let them go behold I will smite all thy borders with frogs'.'

LIZZIE starts to write a list.

LIZZIE: Frogs.

PREACHER: And the Lord did it. And Pharoah said, 'Verily Lord, I will let them go.' But he lied and did not free the people of Israel. So the Lord brought down a plague of lice and great swarms of flies and a plague of boils.

LIZZIE: Boils? Euch!

PREACHER: And yet and still Pharoah lied and would not set my people free. And the Lord sent thunder and hail and the fire ran along upon the ground there was darkness over the land of Egypt, even darkness which may be felt.

LIZZIE: Marguerite.

MARGUERITE: Ssh.

LIZZIE: But listen.

PREACHER: And he sent a plague of locusts and finally the Lord caused the firstborn children to die. Lord let my people go!

MAMA: Amen!

PREACHER: And now let us speak with the Lord.

They pray.

LIZZIE continues writing her list.

LIZZIE: Locusts.

MARGUERITE: What're you writing Lizzie?

LIZZIE: It's a list.

MARGUERITE: What for?

LIZZIE: I'm working out when we're going to be free.

MARGUERITE: What are you talking about?

LIZZIE: Well, we had the hailstorms Monday, flies and frogs we got a plenty, three in our class got head lice and Mrs Jameson's eldest, Joby, got killed overseas and he had boils.

MARGUERITE: You're crazy!

LIZZIE: On the back of his neck. So I reckon can't be long now. Just waiting on the locusts.

The PREACHER shakes hands at the door.

PREACHER: Good day Mrs Walker.

MAMA: Good day Reverend.

PREACHER: Good day Lizzie.

LIZZIE: Will be, soon as we spot a locust.

PREACHER: Pardon me?

MARGUERITE: She don't mean nothing sir. Good day sir.

PREACHER: Good day Marguerite.

PREACHER exits.

LIZZIE: I do so too.

MARGUERITE: It was a plague of locusts. Not one!

LIZZIE: Well Mama says I'm a plague and there's only one of me. So soon as I see just one locust my list'll be complete.

MAMA: Marguerite, Lizzie, come on now.

LIZZIE: Marguerite give up arguing with me then and there. I didn't let on a while later that I read about John the Baptist in the wilderness living on wild honey and locusts. I mean, how we going to get free if the folks supposed to be on our side keeps eating up the locusts?

Song: two verses of 'Little David'.

Scene 5

LIZZIE is standing on a stool while MAMA alters the hem of one of MARGUERITE's or CHARLES's hand-me-downs.

MAMA: And she raised herself up in front of this crowd of heckling hostile folks and she fixed them with a look and she said…

SOJOURNER: Children I have come here like the rest of you to hear what I have to say. I've heard tell you'll set fire to the building if a black woman gets to speak. Go ahead if you've a mind. I'll speak on the ashes if necessary. When I was a slave away down there in New York and there was some particularly bad work to be done, some coloured woman was sure to be called on to do it and when I hear that man talking about my people as nearer to animals and only useful as slaves I said to myself – this is the job for me. I am pure African, not one drop of white blood in me and that makes me real proud. The way you white folks behaving you ain't got no cause to be proud.

MAMA: And a voice from the crowd shouted...

WHITE HECKLER: Listen to the storm blowing out there. It is God's wrath come to strike this meeting!

SOJOURNER: Child, don't be scared. You are not going to be harmed. I don't expect God's ever heard tell of you.

MAMA: That didn't quiet him.

WHITE HECKLER: Old woman, do you think your talk of slavery does any good? Why, I don't care any more for your talk than I do for the bite of a flea!

SOJOURNER: Perhaps not, but the Lord willing, I'll keep you scratching.

MAMA: That Sojourner had the measure of him all right.

WHITE HECKLER: We already have a Constitution says 'all men are equal'. So why you going on about rights?

SOJOURNER: Now I hear talk about this Constitution and the right of man. I come up and take hold of this Constitution. It looks mighty big. And I feel for my rights. But they aren't there. Then I say to God, 'God, what ails this Constitution?' and you know what he says to me? God says, 'Sojourner, there's a little weevil in it.'

MAMA: And the thing about weevils is – they very hard to get rid of. Wheat looks fine till you crack it open and looks inside. Then you find the heart eaten out. Now I tell you child, beware of folk with their heart eaten out. All done.

LIZZIE climbs off the stool.

LIZZIE: Now there's several ways to eat out the heart. Take the movies. Me, I used to save up pennies and go every chance I had. Hollywood, California, Sunset Strip – these were powerful magical words conjuring up for me how the world outside our town was. I told Marguerite about it when I got home. She was still out of a job and had taken to going out alone all of a sudden and coming back with bundles hid under her sweater. She was getting awful secretive and if there's one thing I can't abide, it's secrets.

Scene 6

LIZZIE is practising tap-dancing like the movies.

LIZZIE: Hi Marguerite.

MARGUERITE: Hi.

LIZZIE: You been someplace nice?

MARGUERITE: Hm.

LIZZIE: Sky fell in just afore dinnertime.

MARGUERITE: Oh yeah.

LIZZIE: Thirty people injured by falling stars.

MARGUERITE: Really.

LIZZIE: It's like talking to Adam. I'm not keen on snakes though so I keep on trying. What you got under your sweater Marguerite?

MARGUERITE: Nothing.

LIZZIE: Well in that case, if I was you, I'd get on down see the doctor real fast cos you got a bump developing in the wrong place sister.

MARGUERITE: That so.

MARGUERITE opens the tin trunk, slithers something inside and locks it again.

LIZZIE: Hey Marguerite, where'd you find a turtle with no legs?

MARGUERITE: I don't know.

LIZZIE: Where you left it.

No response.

Where you left it, get it? You know Marguerite, I saw this movie and I reckon I know why you can't get a job. See, all the black folks in the movies who wait on table, are house maids and all, well even in the old days, they smile. And when they ain't waiting on tables smiling, they dancing and smiling. Like they advertising toothpaste dawn to dusk. Don't know how they eat their food wearing those big grins – but they don't show you that part. Must be kinda difficult. But if you practised in front of the mirror I'm sure you could learn it.

MARGUERITE: What!

LIZZIE: I should have seen the weather signs but I just ploughed on in. Today I saw this one about Al Jolson. He sings our songs and there was this one Mama would have liked real well, all about his mother.

LIZZIE tap dances and sings, minstrel-style 'Mammee'. She is really enjoying herself.

MARGUERITE: Shut up.

LIZZIE: And there was me thinking I had a future in show business.

MARGUERITE: Don't you ever sing that song.

LIZZIE: What's the matter with you?

MARGUERITE: You ever hear your mother called Mammee?

LIZZIE: No, but…

MARGUERITE: You ever hear any black folks singing that song?

LIZZIE: Well no, but…

MARGUERITE: Swannee River?

LIZZIE: You seen the movie! Why didn't you say so?

MARGUERITE: I seen some white guy blacking his face, making up songs about the brothers and sisters. What he know about being black? He's just making money off of our backs.

LIZZIE: It's only a movie.

MARGUERITE: And the way they tell it, you only some happy grinning nigger!

LIZZIE: Come to think on it, not only did I not know one woman answering to the name of Mammee, but I couldn't recall anyone I'd met smiling that much neither, particularly when they cleaning up someone else's mess. Marguerite?

MARGUERITE: Yes.

LIZZIE: Do they have a lot of black folks in Hollywood, you know, like producers and directors and all?

MARGUERITE: What do you think, dummy?

LIZZIE: (*To audience.*) Dummy huh? When they make us look foolish it's to keep us under and make them look smart, right?

MARGUERITE: Right.

LIZZIE: They shouldn't do that, should they?

MARGUERITE: No, they shouldn't.

LIZZIE: And the only way we can find out and tell it like it is, is to ask, right?

MARGUERITE: Of course.

LIZZIE: And brothers and sisters should be treated with respect.

MARGUERITE: That's right, yes.

LIZZIE: In that case I don't think you ought to call me dummy, and what you got in that box?

MARGUERITE: Corpses.

LIZZIE: What?

MARGUERITE: Corpses.

LIZZIE: Real live corpses?

MARGUERITE: Corpses.

MARGUERITE exits.

LIZZIE: Well, I just contemplating whether to have one of the fainting fits I hear tell white folks so good at. Perhaps my sister taken to murdering awful small people. I feel the spring coiling tighter and all of a sudden I could hear the dogs of evil snapping at our heels. They slipped their chains and running loose. Somebody going to get bit. Top it all Mama comes in yelling…

MAMA: You forgot to feed the chickens!

LIZZIE: And it wasn't even my turn! Outside I made toe patterns in the dust, wondering why I'm always the one getting hollered at. Stayed out there, thinking about running away, till the mocking bird stopped calling, dark was wrapping all around me, and it didn't seem like such a good idea. Maybe I'd go some other time instead.

Song: 'Hush You Bye', hummed through this speech and then sung at the end.

Scene 7

The yard. LIZZIE is sitting over an essay, chewing her pencil. MAMA is sweeping.

LIZZIE: One hot day I was sitting in the yard trying to figure out how to write this essay we'd been given in school. It had a real dumb title. 'My favourite animal.' Well, I didn't have no favourite animal. I didn't mind pigs – they useful garbage disposal sort of creatures, but you can't hug a pig. I was finding it real hard to come up with an animal I could bear writing about when I realised Mama been talking to me.

MAMA: What's the matter, Lizzie, cat got your tongue?

LIZZIE: Cats? Now that's a possibility.

MAMA: You want to know more about cats you should go see Uncle Chrystal. He been training cats long as I can recall.

MAMA laughs and leaves.

Scene 8

LIZZIE: Now my Great Uncle Chrystal was about two hundred years old. Well, anyways he been around for a long time. His full name was Chrystal Obediah Diamond. Some folks said my Great Aunt Esther only married him on account of his fancy name. It did suit him real well cos even now he was so old and crepey his eyes sort of glittered, specially when he got onto the subject of the code for training cats.

UNCLE CHRYSTAL enters and sits with a feather duster and a rubber mouse.

UNCLE: Okay Esther, you get that mouse now. Go got him!

He thwacks thin air with the duster.

LIZZIE: Ever since Great Aunt Esther died all Uncle Chrystal's cats were called Esther. Afternoon Uncle Chrystal.

UNCLE: Who's that?

LIZZIE: It's me. Lizzie.

UNCLE: Nice to see you child. Sit yourself down. Mind out for Esther. She's in training.

LIZZIE: Nice to see you was just a way of talking. Uncle Chrystal was near blind as an owl at midday. How's it going sir?

UNCLE: Well you got to keep to the code, child. I put down the mouse and wriggles the duster near it so old Esther thinks it's moving and then she pounces. And if she carry on lying in the sun and take no notice I thwacks her a blow with the feathers. Like so! Move it Esther!

LIZZIE: Every now and then Esther would come up to the porch for a stroke or some food, Uncle would hit her over the head with the feather duster and she'd wander off looking kinda dazed. But mostly she kept clear and chased blue jays.

UNCLE: Move it, Esther!

LIZZIE: I guess she was trying to get her own back on the feathers. Uncle Chrystal?

UNCLE: Who's that?

LIZZIE: It's me, Lizzie.

UNCLE: That's funny. I had a great niece called Lizzie once.

LIZZIE: Yeah, that's me.

UNCLE: You sure?

LIZZIE: Yeah.

UNCLE: Then, why didn't you say so? You can't tell with cats. You seen that Esther? She round here someplace.

He whirls the duster round his head fighting off imaginary Esthers.

Got you!

LIZZIE: I come to ask about your code for training cats.

UNCLE: That's right.

LIZZIE: Well, does it work?

UNCLE: When they obey it does.

LIZZIE: And when they don't?

UNCLE: You hit em. Whack!

LIZZIE: Is a code sort of like a law, sir?

UNCLE: Yes child. There's good codes and bad codes. And some just goes on going on account of no one shouts loud enough that they wrong.

LIZZIE: How d'you know what to shout?

UNCLE: Well, Esther used to say, on certain nights if you stamp hard enough, shout loud enough and sing home, you can hear the ancestral bones speak their speak. I guess that's how you know. Esther?

LIZZIE: Why all your cats called Esther anyways?

UNCLE: What?

LIZZIE: The name, Esther?

UNCLE: Always been an Esther in the family. Passed the name on down. Now my wife, her granma was an Esther too, from Africa. And she got dealt with by a code.

LIZZIE: What sort of code Uncle?

UNCLE: Well, more of a law I guess. The English who in the business of stealing your African ancestors and selling them for slaves invented it. It sort of got passed on too.

LIZZIE: But what happened to Esther?

UNCLE: One day her master say he selling her daughter away to another plantation.

LIZZIE: Yeah, and...?

UNCLE: Well, this Esther she say no, this child all I got left of family now. So he beat her like a dog.

LIZZIE: What happened?

UNCLE: She died child.

LIZZIE: Did they lock him up?

UNCLE: What for? He own her. He can do what he like.

LIZZIE: But she's a person!

UNCLE: Uh uh. She his property.

LIZZIE: That ain't right.

UNCLE: It the law though. Law say, 'Christians will not be punished for destroying what belongs to them.' He bought her. She his.

LIZZIE: Christians?

UNCLE: They meant white folks.

LIZZIE: But black folks are Christians too.

UNCLE: Depends on who's owning God at the time child. You seen that cat?

LIZZIE: She's in the bushes, back of the yard someplace.

UNCLE: You sure?

LIZZIE: Well I can't see her.

UNCLE: You know, sometimes I have this dream all the Esthers get together and come back, take over my place. And they learned to use the can opener so they gets their own food. Then they lies on my body, so many I just breathe out from their weight and never breathes in again. Don't know why I dream that cos I never once let an Esther sleep on the bed.

LIZZIE: Maybe your code for training cats isn't too good Uncle Chrystal.

UNCLE: She's my cat! I own her and I do what I like!

LIZZIE: As I left, Uncle Chrystal was dozing on the porch, his stick with the feathers still in his hand. Struck me, just cos you're old doesn't mean you know everything, not bone deep anyhow. I went round the back of the yard looking for old Esther. There she was, nose deep in a petunia. She look up, pollen on her whiskers like face powder. She wasn't smiling neither. All the dusty road home I shouted and I stamped and I sang till the ancestral bones spoke their speak.

Song: Last verse of 'Little David'.

Scene 9

It is another day. MARGUERITE is about to go out. LIZZIE is sitting in the kitchen.

LIZZIE: Where're you going Marguerite?

MARGUERITE: Out.

LIZZIE: Sometimes sisters are such a pain. Where out?

MARGUERITE: Downtown.

MARGUERITE puts on her scarf from the costume trunk.

LIZZIE: What to do?

MARGUERITE: March.

LIZZIE: Oh that.

MARGUERITE: You want to come too?

LIZZIE: Uh uh!

MARGUERITE: Bye then.

LIZZIE: Bye.

MARGUERITE exits.

Hey Marguerite, why you put on your best scarf? You going to meet some boy on that march? You going to do kissing and all that stuff? Are you? Are you?

No reply.

No fun teasing some folks. What to do with Marguerite gone. No one to pester. I decides to daydream instead.

LIZZIE turns on the radio, a local station playing Billie Holliday.

Must have been a good coupla hours later I come to and what did I see sitting there in front of me? The key! That's what. The key to Marguerite's tin trunk!

LIZZIE looks around and goes to the trunk. MAMA's voice is heard off.

MAMA: You done your schoolwork yet?

LIZZIE: Yes Mama.

MAMA: What you doing then?

LIZZIE: Nothing much Mama. (*To herself.*) Just finding out about corpses.

As LIZZIE unlocks and opens the trunk a newsflash comes on the radio.

NEWSCASTER: We interrupt this programme to bring you a newsflash. Disturbances have again hit the downtown area as protestors marched on City Hall. Police report rioting broke out during the march and injuries have been sustained on both sides.

During the above LIZZIE starts to pay attention. Though she has seen the contents of the trunk, she closes the lid.

LIZZIE: The sharp crack of bullet hitting bone sped along the street, past the marchers fleeing in all directions, echoed down the empty corridors of City Hall, dodged through the grey green of the swamp, leapt the river, wove along the dirt track, round the corner of the porch, and slid under the kitchen door and into my ears. I knew. Marguerite! No! Marguerite!

During the following speech MARGUERITE appears on stage and mimes the actions. At the sound of the shot she leaves. 'She Know Moon-rise' is hummed.

Her friends say she was happy that day. Smiling. As they marched and sang she danced, waving her banner. She was near the front of the marchers. The police fired three tear gas bombs, even though there was no trouble. And my sister picked one up and threw it back at them. She was no rioter. That moment she was just angry. She threw the gas back and they shot her, and others too. Her friends say she was very tall that day, like her great-great-grandma some say.

Song: Last verse of 'She Know Moon-rise'.

LIZZIE enters running. Her way is blocked by the COP.

No! Let me through! I want my sister! Marguerite! What have you done with her?

COP: Move back! Get this kid outa here!

LIZZIE: I want my sister. You have no right!

LIZZIE raises her arm.

The COP grabs it and twists it.

COP: Halt!

Freeze.

The COP leaves.

LIZZIE: Mama bailed me out of jail the next morning. They let me go but they would not give up Marguerite's body. She was locked in the City Morgue awaiting a post-mortem, they said. That's when they cut up the dead body to see whose fault it was. I could have told them.

Scene 10

LIZZIE paces in circles. MAMA enters. It is night in the kitchen.

MAMA: Child you must get some rest.

LIZZIE: Not until she's buried.

MAMA: It been five nights now Lizzie honey. You going to get sick.

LIZZIE: She ought to be buried.

MAMA: Lizzie child, let it rest now.

LIZZIE: Not until she does. It just not right.

MAMA: Ain't there enough sorrow in this house!

LIZZIE: Mama, I can't sleep. I don't rightly know what to do. I got to figure it out.

MAMA: Marguerite, my baby, she still here with us now, like the other sisters.

LIZZIE: No she aint! She still in a metal drawer in the City Morgue. She's dead but they still holding her prisoner!

MAMA: Child, please. No more.

LIZZIE: Mama, was you taught me my history.

MAMA: That was a long time ago. Lifetime ago.

LIZZIE: No! Tell me again what Sojourner say, Mama.

MAMA: I'm all tired out Lizzie. The misery's in my bones now, Lord knows.

LIZZIE: You tell me Sojourner say, 'If women want any rights...'

MAMA: No, just rest. Just tonight.

LIZZIE: 'If women want any rights more than they got, why don't they just take them and not be talking about it?' Ain't that the truth, Mama?

MAMA: You the only one I got left.

LIZZIE: I know. I'm sorry. Go back to bed Mama.

MAMA: I'll sit up with you.

LIZZIE: All right.

MAMA: Where I can see you.

LIZZIE: (*Covering MAMA.*) Go to sleep.

LIZZIE watches MAMA nodding in the chair, covered with the half-finished quilt, and speaks to herself as she quietly leaves.

Why don't they just take them.

Scene 11

As MAMA sleeps in the chair, the sound of TWO WHITE WOMEN talking.

1: Did you hear?

2: Did you hear?

1: The rioting.

2: Dreadful. Blacks.

1: Looting.

2: Burning.

1: Shooting.

2: Law and order.

1: Getting uppity.

2: Wanting rights.

1: Control.

2: Police.

1: Law

2: Order.

1: Did you hear?

2: Did you hear?

1: Body stolen.

2: Break in.

1: At dawn.

2: Bold as you like.

1: City Morgue.

2: Black body.

1: Rioter.

2: And a woman.

1: Not proper.

2: Outrageous.

1: Learn their place.

2: Learn their place.

Scene 12

MAMA wakes stiffly.

MAMA: Ouch. I too old for this sitting up sleeping game. Lizzie. Lizzie?

LIZZIE enters.

LIZZIE: Here Mama.

MAMA: Child you look like ghosts got you. What you been doing?

LIZZIE: Could I have a cup of milk? I'm real tired Mama.

MAMA: Course child.

LIZZIE: I been to get Marguerite. I been to get my sister.

MAMA: What!

LIZZIE: I said..

MAMA: I hear what you said. Are you crazy? Are you telling me you broke into the morgue and stole your sister's body?

LIZZIE: How could I 'steal' my own sister?

MAMA: How'd you get in? That place locked solid.

LIZZIE: Charles pass on to me some of the skills the army taught him.

MAMA: Did anyone see you? Lord you going to be in big trouble if they did.

LIZZIE: Mama, they ain't that stupid. Trouble's my middle name now I reckon.

MAMA: They going to arrest you.

LIZZIE: I know. Let them.

MAMA: Tell me child.

LIZZIE: Harriet died alone selling vegetables on the street. History books forgot Sojourner. They threw my great-granma's bones in the yard. My sister's going to be treated with respect. She going to be buried proper. And all this stuff along with her.

MAMA: What's that?

LIZZIE: Marguerite called them corpses. It's ornaments she took from white folks houses, from shops and art stores – black boys holding up lamps, book ends made like black women, toasting forks with black grinning faces on their handles. They going to be buried too. We ain't things. We people.

MAMA and LIZZIE move the trunk.

MAMA: It's heavy.

LIZZIE: It would be.

MAMA: Lizzie, stand up a moment.

LIZZIE does so.

You grown. You getting to be real tall – just like…

Song: one verse of 'Let My People Go'.

LIZZIE: I had a great-great-granma. She took Sojourner Truth as her name. I am her great-great-granddaughter. I am Marguerite's sister. I am Mama's daughter. I am Lizzie Walker taking the name of Trouble because of the trouble behind, taking the name of Fighter because of the struggle ahead. I am Lizzie Walker, on my own story, walking my own road. But we treading it together sisters. Been walked before. Be walked again.

Song: Reprise of 'No More Moaning' – up tempo.

The End.

Printed in the USA
CPSIA information can be obtained
at www.ICGtesting.com
LVHW021003171024
794056LV00004B/1308